Thirty–One Days of Prayer

FOR MY CHILDREN

This resource belongs to:

_____

_____

TIFFANY DICKERSON

Table of Contents

Devote yourselves to prayer; stay alert in it with thanksgiving.

COLOSSIANS 4:2

Introduction

From the moment the pregnancy test says "positive" or the adoption agency calls with exciting news or a child joins your family unexpectedly, our children become a living, breathing extension of our hearts. All the dreams we had for ourselves are refocused and multiplied for them. We hope they avoid the mistakes we have made, escape the pain we have felt, and make far better decisions with fewer regrets. And while these hopes are good, ultimately, we must yearn for our children's lives to be a living testimony of the gospel.

As such, there is no greater gift we can give our children than to pray for them. To approach the throne of God on their behalf is to set aside our hopes and dreams for them and replace them with God's plan for their lives. While it is hard to imagine, God truly loves our children more than we do. David reminds us of this truth when he writes, "Your eyes saw me when I was formless; all my days were written in your book and planned before a single one of them began" (Psalm 139:16). God holds our children in the palm of His hand, and He is worthy of our trust as we offer up prayers for their lives.

Prayer is one of God's many good gifts to His people. It is through prayer that God changes our hearts and the hearts of those for whom we are praying. As you come to the Lord on your children's behalf, pray for them and also ask the Lord to help you exhibit all of the characteristics listed in this book. You are your children's greatest role model, no matter how old they get. Your Christlike actions will lead by example. James 5:16 reminds us of the importance of prayer as James, the author, writes, "The prayer of a righteous person is very powerful in its effect." Seek to be the person you pray your children will one day be. The Father will hear your prayers on their behalf, and you will look more and more like Jesus as well. As parents, may we set the example Paul set for us in Colossians 4:2: "Devote yourselves to prayer; stay alert in it with thanksgiving."

I am not praying that you take them out of the world but that you protect them from the evil one. They are not of the world, just as I am not of the world. Sanctify them by the truth; your word is truth.

JOHN 17:15–17

How to Use This Resource

This booklet is designed so that you can return to it over and over again. Whether your children are infants, toddlers, teenagers, or adults, this booklet will help you spend focused time in prayer each day as you pray for their salvation, friends, future or current spouses, wisdom, health, and faithfulness, to name a few.

For thirty-one days, you will focus on thirty-one different attributes, qualities, or character traits taken from the Bible to pray over your children. Each day has one or two Scripture passages to help focus your own heart as you pray. Each day will also include age-appropriate prayer prompts. This is because the prayers we pray for a six-year-old differ greatly from those we pray for a thirty-six-year-old. The first set of prompts will be for those whose children are infants to twelve years old. The second set of prompts will be for those whose children are thirteen years old to adults. Each age group has a page for you to list or journal your prayers for your children. As your children graduate from one age group to the other, we hope this booklet is a reference you can return to in the years ahead. And we hope you can look back over the years and see how God has been faithful to answer so many of your prayers.

As you begin, take a moment to read the verses to the left and pray them over your children. Jesus prayed these on behalf of His disciples shortly before He went to the cross. These men were His earthly children, just as those who follow Him now are His children too. Jesus prayed for them, taught them, and showed them what it meant to be His disciples. He desired the best for them, and He prayed to the Father on their behalf. As parents, we desire the same for our children. Though we cannot shield them from the world, we can trust the Father as we take our children to the throne every day.

DAY I

Salvation

*My sheep hear my voice, I know them, and they follow
me. I give them eternal life, and they will never perish.
No one will snatch them out of my hand.*

JOHN 10:27–28

*Indeed, God is my salvation; I will trust him and not
be afraid, for the Lord, the Lord himself, is my strength
and my song. He has become my salvation.*

ISAIAH 12:2

Younger Children (Infant–12)

Pray that as your children grow, they will
listen to God's voice as He calls them.

Ask the Lord to give your children a
desire to know Him and follow Him.

Pray that your children will receive the salvation
of Jesus and seek to live a life for Him.

Older Children (13–Adult)

Pray that your children realize Jesus is
the only way in this dark world.

Pray they will hear the voice of Christ
calling them to salvation.

Ask the Lord to show your children that the
world has nothing to offer so that they would
seek their strength and identity in Christ alone.

Prayers for Younger Children

Prayers for Older Children

_____

_____

_____

_____

_____

_____

_____

_____

_____

_____

_____

_____

_____

_____

_____

_____

_____

_____

_____

_____

_____

_____

Faithfulness

*Above all, fear the Lord and worship him faithfully with all
your heart; consider the great things he has done for you.*

I SAMUEL 12:24

Younger Children

Ask the Lord to help you model a life
of faithfulness for your children.

Pray your children see the joy found
in a life of faithfulness to the Lord.

Ask the Lord to help you follow Him with
your whole heart as you teach your children
how to worship, read the Bible, and remember
all God has done in their lives. Pray the
Lord would enable you to instill habits of
faithfulness in your children's young lives.

Older Children

Ask the Lord to give each of your children a
heart that is completely devoted to Him.

Pray your children will see a life of
faithfulness modeled by you. Pray that the
habits of faithfulness you exhibit will be an
example to them to develop their own.

Pray your children will recall the great
things God has done for them and
cultivate a heart of faithfulness.

Prayers for Younger Children

Prayers for Older Children

Love

I pray that he may grant you, according to the riches of his glory, to be strengthened with power in your inner being through his Spirit, and that Christ may dwell in your hearts through faith. I pray that you, being rooted and firmly established in love, may be able to comprehend with all the saints what is the length and width, height and depth of God's love, and to know Christ's love that surpasses knowledge, so that you may be filled with all the fullness of God.

EPHESIANS 3:16–19

Younger Children

Pray that you will exhibit love for God
and others in front of your children.

Ask the Lord to give your children a
desire to love God and others.

As your children grow, pray they will be rooted
and firmly established in Christ's love.

Older Children

Pray your children know that true and
absolute love comes only from God.

Ask the Lord to give your children
hearts to love God and love others.

Pray your children will know the love of
Christ that surpasses all knowledge.

Prayers for Younger Children

Prayers for Older Children

Protection

The one who lives under the protection of the Most High dwells in the shadow of the Almighty. I will say concerning the Lord, who is my refuge and my fortress, my God in whom I trust: He himself will rescue you from the bird trap, from the destructive plague. He will cover you with his feathers; you will take refuge under his wings. His faithfulness will be a protective shield.

PSALM 91:1–4

Younger Children

As you pray for protection over your children, ask the Lord to cover them with His wings of refuge — that they will know His presence even at a young age.

Pray that you will model a heart that depends on God and entrusts your family in the shadow of the Almighty.

Ask the Lord to give you a heart that willingly gives your children to the Lord so that they may go and serve wherever He calls them as they grow, knowing His faithfulness will be their shield.

Older Children

As your older children go out with friends, begin driving, or leave the nest, praying for their protection never ends. Pray for your own heart to trust the faithful shield of the Lord over their lives.

Ask the Father to be their refuge and fortress when life seems difficult, confusing, or painful.

Pray your children have hearts that trust the Lord and His plan for their lives. Whether He sends them to a city or continent far away, pray they will rest in the shadow of the Almighty.

Prayers for Younger Children

Prayers for Older Children

Obedience

I will give you a new heart and put a new spirit within you; I will remove your heart of stone and give you a heart of flesh. I will place my Spirit within you and cause you to follow my statutes and carefully observe my ordinances.

EZEKIEL 36:26–27

Younger Children

As your children grow, ask the Lord to give them
each a new heart that desires to obey Him.

Pray that your children will grow to
love the ordinances and statutes of the
Lord and obey them joyfully.

Ask the Lord to give your children each a heart
that is obedient to Him first and foremost and
one that also overflows with obedience to you,
as a parent, and other authority figures.

Older Children

Ask the Father to give your children hearts to
be obedient to whatever He calls them to do.

Pray that your children will love the ordinances
and statutes of the Lord, obey them joyfully, and
remember they are not burdensome (1 John 5:3).

Ask the Lord to give your children each a
heart that is obedient to Him above all else
and one that overflows with obedience to the
authority figures in their lives so that they
will be a living example of the gospel.

Prayers for Younger Children

Prayers for Older Children

_____

_____

_____

_____

_____

_____

_____

_____

_____

_____

_____

_____

_____

_____

_____

_____

_____

_____

_____

_____

_____

_____

_____

Friends and Influences

How happy is the one who does not walk in the advice of the wicked or stand in the pathway with sinners or sit in the company of mockers! Instead, his delight is in the Lord's instruction, and he meditates on it day and night.

PSALM 1:1–2

Younger Children

Pray for your children's current and future
friends. Pray they will be godly influences
on your children's lives. Pray that your
children will be godly friends to others.

Pray for your children's discernment to stay away
from possible friends and influences who would
lead them down a wicked and destructive path.

Ask the Lord to give each of your children
a heart that loves the Bible and uses
what it says to make godly friends.

Older Children

Pray for your children's discernment as they
make friends in their teenage and adult years.
Ask the Lord to keep them out of the company
of those who could lead them astray.

Pray that your children meditate on the Lord's
instruction from the Bible before they seek
counsel from friends. Pray that their friends
love the Lord and provide godly counsel.

Pray for your children to be godly friends to
others. Ask the Lord to use your children to
help other friends come to know Him.

Prayers for Younger Children

Prayers for Older Children

Wisdom

Now if any of you lacks wisdom, he should ask God—who gives
to all generously and ungrudgingly—and it will be given to him.

JAMES 1:5

For the Lord gives wisdom; from his mouth
come knowledge and understanding.

PROVERBS 2:6

Younger Children

As your children mature, pray they grow in wisdom just as Jesus did when He was a child (Luke 2:52).

The Lord promises that He will give wisdom to those who ask. As your children grow and learn to pray, ask for this wisdom on their behalf. Pray they will begin praying for wisdom at a young age themselves.

Pray that the Lord gives you great wisdom as you raise your children to love Him.

Older Children

Pray that your children will ask the Lord for wisdom and seek to follow it in every stage of life.

Ask the Lord to give your children wisdom, which will help them grow in knowledge and understanding of who He is and what He wants for their lives.

Pray your children seek the Lord in prayer and regular Bible reading. Pray that they realize those are the only places they will find true wisdom.

Prayers for Younger Children

Prayers for Older Children

Purity

And I pray this: that your love will keep on growing in knowledge and every kind of discernment, so that you may approve the things that are superior and may be pure and blameless in the day of Christ.

PHILIPPIANS 1:9–10

God, create a clean heart for me and renew a steadfast spirit within me.

PSALM 51:10

Younger Children

Begin praying now for your young children's purity as they live in a world that cheapens and diminishes it. Pray they will stand firm and seek your counsel as they are exposed to things of this world and have questions. Pray that your home is an open door for discussion that points them to Jesus.

Pray for your children's purity of heart, soul, mind, and body. Pray they have a desire to be pure and blameless before the Father.

Pray that you will set an example of purity in your own marriage or as a single parent. Ask the Father to give you a pure and blameless heart so that you can lead your children by example and through open conversations.

Older Children

Pray for your children's purity of heart, soul, mind, and body. Pray that they pursue purity while remembering that it is Christ who ultimately makes us pure and blameless, and He gives us grace and forgiveness to cover every sin.

Pray that each of your married children will seek to be pure and blameless within their marriages so that they love, respect, and trust their spouse. Pray their pure marriage perseveres and is an example of Christ's pure and sacrificial love for His bride, the Church.

In a world that devalues purity at every turn, pray that your children seek the Lord for a clean heart and renewed spirit in the Lord. Pray that they set their "minds on things above, not on earthly things" (Colossians 3:2).

Prayers for Younger Children

Prayers for Older Children

Speech

*May the words of my mouth and the meditation of my heart
be acceptable to you, Lord, my rock and my Redeemer.*

PSALM 19:14

*Let your speech always be gracious, seasoned with salt, so
that you may know how you should answer each person.*

COLOSSIANS 4:6

Younger Children

Ask the Lord to make your speech to your children kind, gracious, and God-honoring. Pray that your speech will be an example as your children learn to speak and as they begin speaking up at school, sports, church, etc.

Pray that your children's speech will come from hearts driven by love for Jesus, as Matthew 12:34 states, "For the mouth speaks from the overflow of the heart."

Pray that your children will be slow to speak and quick to listen (James 1:19). Pray that their speech will be an offering that is pleasing to the Lord even during their younger years.

Older Children

In a world that uses words as a weapon, pray that the Lord will give your children hearts devoted to Him so that their words overflow with graciousness and kindness.

Pray that your children's speech will be so radically different from the world that others are drawn to Christ.

Pray that your children will be slow to speak and quick to listen (James 1:19). Pray that their speech will be an offering that is pleasing to the Lord.

Prayers for Younger Children

Prayers for Older Children

Conduct

But as the one who called you is holy, you also are to be holy in all your conduct; for it is written, Be holy, because I am holy.

1 PETER 1:15–16

Don't let anyone despise your youth, but set an example for the believers in speech, in conduct, in love, in faith, and in purity.

1 TIMOTHY 4:12

Younger Children

Pray that your conduct sets an example of
holiness for your watching children.

As your children grow, pray they model
good conduct and behavior to others
as a way to worship the Lord.

Pray that your children will be an example
to other believers with their conduct.
Pray they "adopt the same attitude as that
of Christ Jesus" (Philippians 2:5).

Older Children

Ask the Lord to give each of your children a
heart to have conduct that is above reproach.

Pray that your children will be an example
to other believers with their conduct. Pray
they "adopt the same attitude as that
of Christ Jesus" (Philippians 2:5).

God calls believers to be holy as He is holy.
Pray that your children walk closely with the
Lord so that their conduct looks more and
more like Him with each passing year.

Prayers for Younger Children

Prayers for Older Children

_____

_____

_____

_____

_____

_____

_____

_____

_____

_____

_____

_____

_____

_____

_____

_____

_____

_____

_____

_____

_____

_____

_____

Hope

We have this hope as an anchor for the soul, firm and secure. It enters the inner sanctuary behind the curtain. Jesus has entered there on our behalf as a forerunner, because he has become a high priest forever . . .

HEBREWS 6:19–20A

Therefore, with your minds ready for action, be sober-minded and set your hope completely on the grace to be brought to you at the revelation of Jesus Christ.

1 PETER 1:13

Younger Children

Ask the Lord to anchor your soul in hope
as you teach your children to find hope in
Christ in our increasingly dark world.

As your children grow, pray that they will see
Christ as their only hope, both now and forever.

When your children face difficult seasons, ask
the Lord to set your children's hope on Jesus.
Pray that hope in Christ anchors their souls
and they rest firm and secure in Him.

Older Children

There are many things that vie for our
children's souls; pray that the Lord would give
them hope as an anchor for their souls.

Pray that Christ would fill your children's
hearts and they would rest firm and secure
in the hope only He can provide.

Though our world is filled with darkness
and chaos, we have hope in Christ's return.
Pray your children will set their hope on
the glorious return of our Savior.

Prayers for Younger Children

Prayers for Older Children

DAY 12

Peace

*You will keep the mind that is dependent on you in perfect
peace, for it is trusting in you. Trust in the Lord forever, because
in the Lord, the Lord himself, is an everlasting rock!*

ISAIAH 26:3–4

*Peace I leave with you. My peace I give to you. I do not give to you
as the world gives. Don't let your heart be troubled or fearful.*

JOHN 14:27

Younger Children

Ask the Lord to help you model peace for your children by having a mind that is dependent on the Lord.

Our children feel anxiety from their parents and the world around them. Pray that from a young age, they would begin to turn to God through prayer, worship, and Scripture memory when their hearts are anxious and need peace. Pray their hearts and minds dwell on Jesus.

Jesus promised to give us His peace. This comes from the presence of the Holy Spirit in our lives. Pray that your children come to know Jesus, if they have not already, so they can experience this peace. If they have experienced salvation, pray they will rest in the peace of the Holy Spirit in their lives so they will not be troubled or fearful.

Older Children

Ask the Lord to help you model peace for your children by having a mind that is dependent on the Lord. Even as they grow older, you are their greatest role model for a life lived for Christ.

Our world vies for the trust of our children, young and old. Ask the Lord to help your children place their trust in Christ alone. He is the only Rock on which they can stand and find true peace.

Jesus promised to give us His peace. This comes from the presence of the Holy Spirit in our lives. Pray that your children come to know Jesus, if they have not yet, so they can experience this peace. If they have experienced salvation, pray they will rest in the peace of the Holy Spirit in their lives so that they will not be troubled or fearful.

Prayers for Younger Children

Prayers for Older Children

Thankfulness

*Rejoice always, pray constantly, give thanks in everything;
for this is God's will for you in Christ Jesus.*

I THESSALONIANS 5:16–18

*The Lord is my strength and my shield; my heart
trusts in him, and I am helped. Therefore my heart
celebrates, and I give thanks to him with my song.*

PSALM 28:7

Younger Children

Ask the Lord to help you cultivate a home filled with thankfulness for all He provides through salvation and provision for your home and family.

Continue to pray for the salvation of your young children. As they understand what it truly means, pray they have hearts that radiate thankfulness for what Jesus has done for them.

Ask the Lord to give your children hearts that are thankful in all things. Pray they value all the Lord provides and that their thankfulness spills into the lives of others.

Older Children

Ask the Lord to help you set an example of thankfulness for your children. Whether they still live at home or only return for visits, pray that your example of thankfulness spills over into their lives.

Pray that your children will have hearts that trust in the Lord and overflow with thankfulness for their salvation.

As your children decide their career paths and follow their hopes and dreams, pray they will live out the will of God in all they do — rejoicing always, praying constantly, and giving thanks in all things.

Prayers for Younger Children

Prayers for Older Children

Patience

*Patience is better than power, and controlling
one's emotions, than capturing a city.*

PROVERBS 16:32

*Therefore I, the prisoner in the Lord, urge you to walk worthy of
the calling you have received, with all humility and gentleness,
with patience, bearing with one another in love, making every
effort to keep the unity of the Spirit through the bond of peace.*

EPHESIANS 4:1–3

Younger Children

Pray that the Lord will help you exhibit patience to your children as you interact with them and others.

Pray for teachable moments with your children so that they can learn how to feel their emotions without being ruled by them. Pray the Lord uses patience in their lives to exhibit His peace.

Pray that the Lord gives your children a heart to bear with others in patience and love.

Older Children

Pray that your children live lives worthy of the calling they have received in Christ by living a life that exhibits patience to fellow believers and to a lost world.

Ask the Lord to show your children that patience is worth the effort as they seek to live a life of peace among others.

Pray that the Lord gives your children a heart to bear with others in patience and love.

Prayers for Younger Children

Prayers for Older Children

Joy

You reveal the path of life to me; in your presence is
abundant joy; at your right hand are eternal pleasures.

PSALM 16:11

Younger Children

Ask the Lord to help you radiate joy to your children.
This is not a false or fake happiness. Allow them to
see all your emotions, but pray that joy in the Lord
is the overarching characteristic they see in you.

As your children grow, pray they find abundant joy as they
sing to Him, pray to Him, and worship Him with others.

Pray that your children's lives will be marked by joy
because they know Jesus as their Savior and have the
joyful expectation of worshiping Him forever.

Older Children

Do your children see joy in your life? Pray that the
Lord gives you abundant joy in your walk with Him
and that it spills over into your children's lives, whether
they live in your home or across the country.

As your children find their way in this world and search
for who they are meant to be, ask the Lord to show them
that the only path that leads to life is the one that leads
to Jesus. Only on that path will they find true joy.

Ask the Lord to show your children that joy in the
Lord comes from salvation. It does not mean they are
happy all the time, but they find joy as they hope for
the eternal pleasures around the throne of God.

Prayers for Younger Children

Prayers for Older Children

Love for God's Word

Your word is a lamp for my feet and a light on my path.

PSALM 119:105

Your word is completely pure, and your servant loves it.

PSALM 119:140

Younger Children

Pray that your love for God's Word would spill over
into your children's lives. Ask the Lord to give you
a love for Scripture so that you can share it with
your children in every aspect of your family's life.

As your children grow, ask the Lord to
give them a heart that wants to read the
Bible and memorize Scripture.

Pray that your children will love the Word of
God and see from a young age that it alone is the
absolute truth upon which to build their life.

Older Children

Pray that your love for God's Word would spill over
into your children's lives. Ask the Lord to give you
a love for Scripture so that you can share it with
your children, no matter their age or stage of life.

As your children work through school or their jobs,
pray that God uses the Bible to light their path and
show them how to live for Jesus in a dark world.

There are many opinions and thoughts vying for
our attention; ask the Lord to show your children
that His Word alone is pure and absolute truth.
Pray that they truly love the Word of the Lord.

Prayers for Younger Children

Prayers for Older Children

Humility

Do nothing out of selfish ambition or conceit, but in humility consider others as more important than yourselves. Everyone should look not to his own interests, but rather to the interests of others. Adopt the same attitude as that of Christ Jesus.

PHILIPPIANS 2:3–5

Younger Children

Is your life marked by humility? Ask the Lord to help you model humility to your children by putting the interests of others before your own.

Pray that your children will come to know Jesus as their Lord and Savior. As they grow to be more and more like Him, pray that their attitudes would be marked by humility, just like their Savior.

Pray for opportunities for your family to model humility to others through acts of service in your community, hospitality to neighbors, and kindness to strangers.

Older Children

Is your life marked by humility? Ask the Lord to help you model humility to your children by putting the interests of others before your own.

In a world where people value ambition and pride in all they do, pray that your children will desire to be like Christ and put others first, whether they are in school or the workforce.

Pray that your children will have opportunities to model a Christlike attitude through acts of service in their community, hospitality to neighbors, and kindness to strangers.

Prayers for Younger Children

Prayers for Older Children

Confidence in Christ

The person who trusts in the Lord, whose confidence indeed is the Lord, is blessed.

JEREMIAH 17:7

I am sure of this, that he who started a good work in you will carry it on to completion until the day of Christ Jesus.

PHILIPPIANS 1:6

Younger Children

Ask the Lord to help you display confidence
in your salvation to your children.

As your children grow, pray that as a
family, you seek the Lord in prayer together
and confidently trust in His care and
plan for your lives when trials come.

When the enemy tries to steal your children's
innocence, joy, and hope, pray that they turn to
Christ as their strength and foundation to live
their lives for Him in confidence and boldness.

Older Children

Ask the Lord to give your children hearts
that trust Christ in all they do. Pray that
they cling to His promises and find their
confidence in Him until He returns.

Pray that your children see that true blessing
comes from a life that is sold out to Christ
and confident in His work on the cross.

When the world tries to steal your teenage or adult
children's innocence, joy, and hope, pray that they
turn to Christ as their strength and foundation to
live their lives for Him in confidence and boldness.

Prayers for Younger Children

Prayers for Older Children

Compassion

Love one another deeply as brothers and sisters.
Take the lead in honoring one another.

ROMANS 12:10

And be kind and compassionate to one another, forgiving
one another, just as God also forgave you in Christ.

EPHESIANS 4:32

Younger Children

Do you show compassion to others? Ask the
Lord to give you a compassionate heart that
shows kindness and grace to others so that your
children have a living example of this trait.

In a "me first" society, pray that your children seek
to honor others by placing others before themselves.

Ask the Lord to give your children
compassionate hearts that are quick to
forgive and reflect Jesus to others.

Older Children

In a "me first" society, pray that your children seek
to honor others by placing others before themselves.

Ask the Lord to give your children
compassionate hearts that are quick to
forgive and reflect Jesus to others.

Pray that your children's involvement in their local
church would be filled with compassion and the desire
to love one another well in front of a watching world.
Pray the compassion they show to fellow believers
would spill over into every aspect of their life.

Prayers for Younger Children

Prayers for Older Children

Health and Safety

I will both lie down and sleep in peace, for you alone, Lord, make me live in safety.

PSALM 4:8

But the Lord is faithful; he will strengthen you and guard you from the evil one.

2 THESSALONIANS 3:3

Younger Children

Ask the Lord to help you entrust the health and safety of your children to His capable hands. Pray that He helps you remember that He loves them even more than you do, and He will guard and protect them. Pray for His loving protection over their health and safety.

As your children grow, pray they will turn to the Lord in prayer and seek comfort from Him for even the smallest "boo-boo." Pray that they realize the Lord is their help for health and safety.

Pray that your children seek God as their refuge to strengthen and guard them against all the arrows the enemy will throw at them as they grow.

Older Children

Ask the Lord to help you entrust the health and safety of your children to His capable hands. Pray that He helps you remember that He loves them even more than you do, and He will guard and protect them.

When hard seasons come for your children concerning their health and safety, pray that they will turn to the Lord in prayer and seek comfort from Him. Pray they realize that the Lord is their help in all things, and His purposes will prevail.

Pray that your children seek God as their refuge to strengthen and guard them against all the arrows the enemy will throw at them as they navigate a lost world.

Prayers for Younger Children

Prayers for Older Children

Courage

Above all, be strong and very courageous to observe carefully the whole instruction my servant Moses commanded you. Do not turn from it to the right or the left, so that you will have success wherever you go. This book of instruction must not depart from your mouth; you are to meditate on it day and night so that you may carefully observe everything written in it. For then you will prosper and succeed in whatever you do.

JOSHUA 1:7–8

Younger Children

Ask the Lord to give you opportunities to show your children that courage comes from knowing and trusting Him. Pray they see courage in your life because you have the Word hidden in your heart.

When your children face "monsters under their bed" or bullies at school, pray that the Lord is their courage and strength. Pray they see that a life that loves Jesus and His commands is what gives them the courage to face their foes, real or imagined.

Pray that your children know and love their Bibles. Ask the Lord to give each of them a heart that meditates on His Word. Pray they remember the Word is the sword of the Spirit and how we courageously fight our battles (Ephesians 6:17).

Older Children

Our culture continually wages war in our children's lives to seek control of their hearts. Pray they stay strong and courageous in the face of sin. Pray they look to Jesus and do not turn to the left or right.

Success in our world is defined by material possessions and career ladder climbing. Success in God's kingdom is defined by being courageous to cling to the Word of God. Pray that your children observe what Scripture says and find their success in a life that is sold out to Christ in all they do.

Pray that your children know and love their Bibles. Ask the Lord to give each of them a heart that meditates on His Word. Pray that they remember the Word is the sword of the Spirit and the tool we deploy to courageously fight our battles (Ephesians 6:17).

Prayers for Younger Children

Prayers for Older Children

Life of Prayer

Rejoice in hope; be patient in affliction; be persistent in prayer.

ROMANS 12:12

Devote yourselves to prayer; stay alert in it with thanksgiving.

COLOSSIANS 4:2

Younger Children

Do your children see you pray? Your prayer life is
the greatest example they will have in this important
practice. Ask the Lord to make you faithful in prayer and
diligent in pointing your children to talking to God.

Ask the Lord to give your children hearts that are
sensitive to prayer. When they get hurt or have
a bad day at school, pray that their hearts would
immediately turn to Jesus for help and comfort.

Pray that you and your children will live lives
marked by prayers of thanksgiving as you
rejoice in all the Lord has done for you.

Older Children

Would your children describe you as a prayer warrior?
It's never too late to start. As your children get older, share
with them the specific prayers you pray for them. Whether
you live near or far from them, ask the Lord to help you be
diligent in pointing your children to the Lord in prayer.

Pray that your children will be devoted to prayer. When
the cares of this world overwhelm them, ask the Father
to prompt them to be in prayer to find their hope.

Pray that your children's lives would be marked by
thanksgiving because they are persistent and alert in prayer.

Prayers for Younger Children

Prayers for Older Children

Discernment

*Do not be conformed to this age, but be transformed by
the renewing of your mind, so that you may discern what
is the good, pleasing, and perfect will of God.*

ROMANS 12:2

*Let no one deceive you with empty arguments, for God's wrath is coming
on the disobedient because of these things. Therefore, do not become
their partners. For you were once darkness, but now you are light in the
Lord. Walk as children of light—for the fruit of the light consists of all
goodness, righteousness, and truth—testing what is pleasing to the Lord.*

EPHESIANS 5:6–10

Younger Children

Ask the Lord to give you a heart of discernment to know what influences to allow in the lives of your children. And though they may be angry when they cannot see a certain movie, play a particular game, or have a cell phone, pray the Lord uses you to teach them the wisdom behind such decisions.

Pray that your children's minds will be continually renewed through reading the Word, prayer, worship music, and gospel-centered community so that they can clearly discern what God wants for their lives and who they are called to be in Christ.

Ask the Lord to give your children a desire to know Jesus and seek His forgiveness so that they can live as shining lights in this world, able to discern empty arguments and seek righteousness and truth.

Older Children

As the world battles for control of your teenage or adult children's hearts, pray they will "not be conformed to this age" (Romans 12:2). Pray they will stand firm in the truths of Scripture and discern the will of the Father.

Pray that your children's minds will be continually renewed through reading the Word, prayer, and gospel-centered community so that they can clearly discern what God wants for their lives and who they are called to be in Christ.

Ask the Lord to give each of your children a heart to know and serve Jesus so that they can live as shining lights in this dark world, able to discern empty arguments and seek righteousness and truth.

Prayers for Younger Children

Prayers for Older Children

_____

_____

_____

_____

_____

_____

_____

_____

_____

_____

_____

_____

_____

_____

_____

_____

_____

_____

_____

_____

_____

_____

_____

_____

_____

Forgiveness

Therefore, as God's chosen ones, holy and dearly loved, put on compassion, kindness, humility, gentleness, and patience, bearing with one another and forgiving one another if anyone has a grievance against another. Just as the Lord has forgiven you, so you are also to forgive.

COLOSSIANS 3:12–13

Younger Children

Ask the Lord to give you a heart that models forgiveness. Pray that your children see your forgiveness toward those who hurt you.

Pray for teachable moments with your children to talk about forgiveness and why it is important. From sibling arguments to possible bullies at school, ask the Lord to show you and your children how to forgive others just as Jesus forgave all sin on the cross.

Pray that each of your children will be marked by a forgiving spirit, and pray that others will see compassion, kindness, humility, gentleness, and patience in their lives as a result.

Older Children

Pray that your children will readily forgive others just as Jesus forgave us while He hung on the cross. Pray they will let go of all grievances so that they can live lives of joy.

In a world that celebrates anger, resentment, and bitterness, pray that your children will be clothed in compassion, kindness, humility, gentleness, and patience as they forgive others.

Pray that as your children go to school or work, they will remember they are God's chosen ones. Pray they represent Christ to a dark world and that they are known as people with a forgiving and gracious spirit.

Prayers for Younger Children

Prayers for Older Children

Resist Temptation

*No temptation has come upon you except what is common to
humanity. But God is faithful; he will not allow you to be
tempted beyond what you are able, but with the temptation he will
also provide the way out so that you may be able to bear it.*

I CORINTHIANS 10:13

*For we do not have a high priest who is unable to
sympathize with our weaknesses, but one who has been
tempted in every way as we are, yet without sin.*

HEBREWS 4:15

Younger Children

As you battle temptation in your own life, ask the Lord to help you flee it and display to your children, in age-appropriate ways, how God always provides a way out.

Pray for teachable moments when your children are young that you can talk about what temptation is and how they can turn to the Lord to help battle against it.

Ask the Lord to help you teach your children that Jesus knows and understands everything that tempts us because He was tempted too. Pray that your children see how Jesus handled His own temptations with the power of God's Word, and pray that they would hide His Word in their hearts as well.

Older Children

Temptation abounds for teenagers and adults today. Pray that your children will draw near to Jesus and hide the Word of God in their hearts so that they can battle against temptation with Scripture just as Jesus did in the wilderness (Matthew 4:1–11).

Pray that your children realize God always provides a way out. It might not be the easy way, but it is His way. Pray that they remember God's faithfulness to His children.

When your children feel like no one understands them or what they are dealing with in life, pray they remember that Jesus dealt with every kind of temptation known to man and, because of this, can sympathize with anything they may be facing. Pray that they seek Jesus for comfort and direction.

Prayers for Younger Children

Prayers for Older Children

Purpose and Calling

Let the word of Christ dwell richly among you, in all wisdom teaching and admonishing one another through psalms, hymns, and spiritual songs, singing to God with gratitude in your hearts. And whatever you do, in word or in deed, do everything in the name of the Lord Jesus, giving thanks to God the Father through him.

COLOSSIANS 3:16–17

Younger Children

Our success-driven culture tells children from a young age to find their career and calling in life. Pray that the Lord helps you instill His Word in your children's hearts so that they know their purpose and calling is to be what God wants for their lives first and foremost.

Pray that the Lord gives your children hearts that desire to worship Him in all they do through the Word, worship, and gospel-centered community.

Pray that your children will do everything in their lives for the glory of Jesus.

Older Children

As your teenagers contemplate their future or your adult children focus on a career path, pray that their purpose and calling come from what the Lord wants for their lives and not what the world tells them is important.

Pray that your children will have hearts that desire to serve the Lord first and foremost through the Word, worship, and gospel-centered community.

Pray that your children will do everything in their lives for the glory of Jesus.

Prayers for Younger Children

Prayers for Older Children

Spouse or Future Spouse

*Love the Lord your God with all your heart, with
all your soul, and with all your mind.*

MATTHEW 22:37

For we walk by faith, not by sight.

2 CORINTHIANS 5:7

Younger Children

If you are married, model prayer for your spouse in front of your children. Pray that they see their parents prioritize prayer for one another and their marriage. If you are not married, model what it looks like to pray for a future spouse or pray for contentment in your present stage of life.

Pray that each of your children would grow up to marry a spouse who loves the Lord with all of his or her heart, soul, and mind.

Pray that your children's future spouses will be quick to repent of sin and will choose to wholeheartedly live for the Lord.

Older Children

If your children are not yet married, pray they will each seek a mate who loves Jesus. Pray they will look at the beauty of the person's heart and not focus on the fleeting beauty of this world.

If your children are not yet married, pray that they will each grow up to marry a spouse who loves the Lord with all of their heart, soul, and mind. If your children are already married, pray that each of their spouses will continually grow in their relationship with the Lord.

Whether your children are married yet or not, pray that each of their spouses or future spouses will be quick to repent of sin and will choose to live for the Lord wholeheartedly.

Prayers for Younger Children

Prayers for Older Children

_____

_____

_____

_____

_____

_____

_____

_____

_____

_____

_____

_____

_____

_____

_____

_____

_____

_____

_____

_____

_____

_____

_____

_____

_____

_____

_____

_____

_____

Honesty and Integrity

*Indeed, we are giving careful thought to do what is right,
not only before the Lord but also before people.*

2 CORINTHIANS 8:21

*The one who lives with integrity lives securely, but
whoever perverts his ways will be found out.*

PROVERBS 10:9

Younger Children

Pray that you model a life of honesty and integrity
before your children at home, at church, in your work,
and anywhere else you might have influence.

Ask the Lord to give your children hearts that desire
to do what is right before God and others.

Pray that your children will live lives that are secure in
integrity, and though it may be painful, pray they will
be found out if they lie so that they may seek repentance,
draw near to the Lord, and walk in honesty.

Older Children

In a world that dismisses honesty and integrity in an effort to
gain notoriety and wealth, pray that your children will not
succumb to this false narrative. Pray that their hearts would
value truth and seek the Author of truth with their lives.

Ask the Lord to give your children hearts that desire
to do what is right before God and others. Pray that
their character behind closed doors and in front of
others is consistently honest and filled with integrity.

Pray that your children will live lives that are secure in
integrity, and though it may be painful, pray they will
be found out if they lie so that they may seek repentance,
draw near to the Lord, and walk in honesty.

Prayers for Younger Children

Prayers for Older Children

Perseverance and Endurance

*Consider it a great joy, my brothers and sisters, whenever you
experience various trials, because you know that the testing of your
faith produces endurance. And let endurance have its full effect,
so that you may be mature and complete, lacking nothing.*

JAMES 1:2–4

*His divine power has given us everything required
for life and godliness through the knowledge of him
who called us by his own glory and goodness.*

2 PETER 1:3

Younger Children

As your children experience trials and difficulties, pray that you can show them how God provides His children with the endurance they need to face life.

Pray that your children will know the Lord deeply and realize from a young age that God has given them everything they need to live their lives for Him.

Pray that the Lord will give your children the strength to persevere against the evil one and his schemes. Pray that their endurance will produce maturity and deeper faith.

Older Children

Ask the Lord to give your children hearts that love Him deeply. Pray that in every trial, they know that He has given them everything they need to live a life of endurance and godliness for Him.

Pray that the Lord will give your children the strength to persevere against the evil one and his schemes. Pray that their endurance will produce maturity and deeper faith.

As many outside influences try to steal your children's hearts and minds, pray that your children will persevere in trial and difficulty because they know and trust Jesus and His divine power.

Prayers for Younger Children

Prayers for Older Children

Contentment

Keep your life free from the love of money. Be satisfied with what you have, for he himself has said, I will never leave you or abandon you.

HEBREWS 13:5

But godliness with contentment is great gain. For we brought nothing into the world, and we can take nothing out.

I TIMOTHY 6:6–7

Younger Children

Are you satisfied with what you have? Is your life marked by excess? Pray that your life will model contentment for your children in how you spend money, care for the place you live, and share what you have with others.

Ask the Lord to give your children hearts that learn from an early age that true satisfaction comes from Jesus, who provides for our needs and promises never to leave or abandon us.

Pray that your children will learn that godliness is the greatest gain in life. Pray for teachable moments when you can show them that "stuff" is fleeting, but a heart that loves the Lord is what lasts.

Older Children

Are you satisfied with what you have? Is your life marked by excess? Even as your children become adults, pray that your life will model contentment for them in how you spend money, care for the place you live, and share what you have with others.

In a world that loves "stuff," pray that your children will learn that godliness is the greatest gain in life. Pray that they will see material wealth as fleeting and have hearts that love and serve the Lord with all their possessions.

Ask the Lord to give your children hearts that are satisfied in Him alone. Pray they rely on the promise that He will never leave or forsake us.

Prayers for Younger Children

Prayers for Older Children

Fruitfulness

Don't be deceived: God is not mocked. For whatever a person sows he will also reap, because the one who sows to his flesh will reap destruction from the flesh, but the one who sows to the Spirit will reap eternal life from the Spirit. Let us not get tired of doing good, for we will reap at the proper time if we don't give up. Therefore, as we have opportunity, let us work for the good of all, especially for those who belong to the household of faith.

GALATIANS 6:7–10

Younger Children

Pray for your children's salvation and that the trappings of this world will not deceive them. If they trust the Lord at a young age, pray that their walks grow deeper year after year as you help them love Jesus more and more.

Pray that your children will reap a harvest of faith and fruitfulness for the kingdom of God in your home, at church, at school, and in hobbies and sports activities.

Pray that other kids will look at your children and already see something different in them. Pray that your children will draw close to the Lord. Pray that they will not grow tired of doing good and being fruitful for the Lord.

Older Children

Pray for your children's relationship with the Lord. For those who don't know Him, pray for their salvation and that they won't be deceived by the trappings of this world. For those who do know Him, pray that their relationship will grow deeper and reap eternal life in the Spirit.

As the world becomes darker and increasingly more difficult for believers, pray that your children will draw close to the Lord and not grow tired of doing good.

Pray that your children will reap a harvest of faith and fruitfulness for the kingdom of God in their home, their church, their community, and their workplace.

Prayers for Younger Children

Prayers for Older Children

_____

_____

_____

_____

_____

_____

_____

_____

_____

_____

_____

_____

_____

_____

_____

_____

_____

_____

_____

_____

_____

_____

_____

_____

Thank you for studying
God's Word with us!

CONNECT WITH US

@thedailygraceco

@dailygracepodcast

CONTACT US

info@thedailygraceco.com

SHARE

#thedailygraceco

VISIT US ONLINE

www.thedailygraceco.com

MORE DAILY GRACE

The Daily Grace App
Daily Grace Podcast